NOT
GUILTY

A CRIMINAL DEFENSE INVESTIGATOR'S GUIDE TO WINNING YOUR CASE

DR. ANTHONY L. ROBBINS

NOT GUILTY:
A Criminal Defense Investigator's Guide to Winning Your Case
Dr. Anthony L. Robbins

Copyright © 2020 by Anthony L. Robbins
Published by Pecan Tree Publishing

Paperback ISBN: 978-1-7358295-4-8
E-book ISBN: 978-1-7358295-5-5

Library of Congress Catalog Number: 2021902433

Cover Design by: Patricia Laurenceau Jean-Louis,
Laurenceau Design Studios
Interior Design by: Jenette Antonio Sityar
Interior Images: Anthony L. Robbins and Envato Elements

Pecan Tree Publishing
www.pecantreebooks.com

New Voices | New Styles | New Vision
Creating a New Legacy of Dynamic Authors and Titles
Hollywood, FL

CHIEF WASHAKIE

1798 – 1900

"It has always been my fervent hope and policy through these long years
to maintain peace and harmony ... It is my earnest prayer that you will
follow the footsteps which I have made for you."

Chief Washakie – February 19, 1900

WYOMING

ABOUT THE AUTHOR

Dr. Anthony L. Robbins, a lifelong resident of South Florida, is the Chief Forensic Criminal Defense Investigator with the firm of Anthony L. Robbins, P.A. He received his undergraduate degree in Legal Studies, and his graduate degree in Criminal Justice. Dr. Robbins is a former member of the City of Miami Civilian Investigative Panel's Complaints Committee where he utilized the specialized training he has received from the Miami-Dade County Police Department Training Bureau as well as the City of Sunrise Police Department Training Unit, and the University of Louisville's Southern Police Institute in the field of Homicide Investigations, Blood Spatter, Latent Print Examination, Crime Scene Investigations and Police-Involved Shootings.

Dr. Robbins is one of the leading experts in his field and is a member of the International Association of Identification, the International Blood Pattern Analysis Association, where he has traveled to Paris, and other countries, for specialized training in the field of Blood Spatter. He is also a member of the International Homicide Investigators Association and the Certified Fraud Examiners Association. Robbins was previously identified by the Eleventh Judicial Circuit Court as one of the first African American males to be designated as a Supervised Visitation Provider in and for Miami-Dade County, Florida.

Dr. Robbins formerly worked in the public sector in the law enforcement field as a State Criminal Investigator and worked in the social service field with the Florida Department of Children and Families, the Miami-Dade County Public Defender's Office and served as a Certified Guardian Ad Litem, investigating best interest cases involving abused and neglected children. Dr. Robbins, is also a member of the 5000 Role Models of Excellence in South Florida.

No stranger to the residents of the City of Miami, his work has led him to receiving proclamations from former Miami-Dade County Mayor Alex Penelas and former City of Miami Mayor Manny Diaz. He was also nominated by former Governor Jeb Bush to serve on the U.S. Selective Service System where Robbins received a Presidential appointment to serve on the board by former U.S. President George W. Bush. He was recognized and honored by former U.S. President Bill Clinton for his work with the American Reads Program and was honored by the late Florida Governor Lawton Chiles for his work within the community. Dr. Robbins has additionally served on the City of Miami Community Relations Board bridging relations between law enforcement and the residents of the City of Miami.

Robbins has dedicated his life to educating, investigating, and advocating for change in the American judicial system where race and social background and cultural misunderstanding have dictated the future of many Americans who have been falsely accused, convicted wrongfully and have had their families shattered. He advocates for the less fortunate ad prides himself on the 13th Amendment of the United States Constitution which states that "Neither slavery nor involuntary servitude, except as a punishment for crime whereof the party shall have been duly convicted, shall exist within the United States, or any place subject to their jurisdiction."

CLIENTS RAVE ABOUT DR. ROBBINS' SUCCESS

SEVER SHERIFF – Attempted Murder - Not Guilty

"I was charged with Attempted Murder in Miami-Dade County, Florida and I owe my life to Dr. Anthony L. Robbins who served as my Criminal Defense Investigator along with my Defense Attorney Mr. Gregory M Iamunno. Dr. Robbins, was able to locate witnesses and find information the police left out of their reports which created reasonable doubt and led to my exoneration. Thanks to Dr. Robbins, I was able to see my babies grow up and experience how great life really is. Dr. Robbins gave me my life back; I was looking at a life sentence."

FREDRICK PARKS - First Degree Murder - Case Dismissed

"I was charged with First Degree Murder and represented by Scott Janowitz who introduced me to Dr. Robbins. As a young man I did not trust my attorney or the criminal justice system. I had been sitting in jail for four years before meeting Dr. Robbins. It was a surprise to see a black man like me who looked like me on my defense team. He gave me a level of assurance that none of my lawyers or my former public defender was able to provide. He gave me hope. He told me that he had a son my age and that he was going to do everything in his power to help me. Shortly after being assigned to my case, Dr. Robbins, was able to find evidence that validated my alibi, subsequently leading to the case being dismissed. Dr. Robbins was the best and his work showed that he is that! I'm walking free today thanks to him."

TRACY SCOTT - Murder Second Degree/ Conspiracy - Nolle Pros

"I have been in and out of the system for years, selling drugs and other things. Being in the streets and knowing game, I can tell you that Anthony Robbins is the real deal. He kicks ass! He was able to get me off using both street and book knowledge. The man is one of the best criminal defense investigators I know; and across Miami everyone knows the work he does. All I can say is thanks my brother."

SAMORIE SINGER - Attempted Murder / Charges Decreased to Aggravated Battery with Deadly Weapon - Probation

"It gives me great pleasure to write this testimonial on behalf of Dr. Anthony Robbins. Although I was sentenced to five years of Reporting Probation, I am grateful because I was originally charged with Attempted Murder. Dr. Robbins put together a great package of investigative findings which helped to mitigate my sentence and get my charges lowered. I was looking at 20 years in prison but thanks to Dr. Robbins' thorough work, I ended up serving no prison time."

ACKNOWLEDGEMENTS

I want to start by giving God the honor and glory for inspiring me with the concept for this book. I am grateful for my wife, my parents and my kids for their continued support.

But none of this would not have been possible without the professional colleagues who helped to develop me into one of the Top Criminal Defense Investigators in the nation. I want to thank my great friends Attorney Rodney B. Robinson and Attorney Gregory M. Iamunno who were two of the first defense attorneys to believe in me and help me craft my trade

I give thanks to the Honorable Judge Jacqueline Schwartz, Honorable Judge Scott Janowitz, Honorable Judge Arthur Taylor as well as the late Miami City Commissioner Arthur Teele, and Former Florida Governor Jeb Bush—to name a few—who were there to assist in jump starting my career.

CONTENTS

FOREWORD

FREEDOM. "The power or right to act, speak, or think as one wants without hindrance or restrain. The state of not being imprisoned or enslaved." (Oxford Dictionary) As an African American male who grew up in Miami, Florida, I was captivated when I discovered that many of my peers were denied the basic right to be free. I grew up in a home where my dad stressed that I had to be the best, that I had to be better than the average guy and 10 times better than my white friends.

Growing up I watched my father befriend judges, prosecutors, doctors, lawyers and even the homeless. Like many young people, I also felt my dad was a sell-out, he was old-fashioned, he didn't understand life and he based everything on how his professional friends felt. My dad believed that everyone was created equal and despite one's professional or cultural background, he treated everyone as if they were on his level.

As a child, and even as I grew into a man, I admired my father; but I also despised him. He would not allow me to do anything. I wasn't allowed to attend parties with my friends. I had to be home before the streetlights came on. He always wanted to know where I was going and who I was going with. It wouldn't be until years later that I would appreciate the teachings and restrictions of my father.

When I started seeing my friends go to prison, get killed on the streets and be beaten by police then I understood why my dad was the way he was and why he shared the advice that he did. Growing up in a law enforcement home was hard, the rules seemed unbearable at times; but I must say that thanks to my dad and those rules I'm alive today. I have never been to jail and after witnessing the way black men are treated in society, I'm able to survive and appreciate FREEDOM because of his experience, wisdom and professional insight.

The U.S. Department of Justice (DOJ) reports 2.2 million people are in our nation's jails and prisons and another 4.5 million people are on probation or parole in the U.S., totaling 6.8 million people, one of every 35 adults. We are the world leader in incarceration. Most of the people incarcerated are poor and Black. I have watched my dad fight for young men and women included in those numbers who otherwise felt no one would represent them favorably. His experience in helping people win their cases is remarkable. His desire to be the best has led to his being listed as one of the Top African American Criminal Defense Investigators in the nation. I have witnessed my father train a multicultural and multi-ethnic gathering of investigators. He does not see color when he's investigating, he sees FREEDOM for his clients. Dad has been trained in social diversity, ritualistic and occult crimes, latent print examination, and blood spatters. His global training in other areas like Homicide Investigations, Police Involved Shootings, Crime Scene Reconstruction is all about the liberty and equitable treatment of those he serves.

If you love and value your FREEDOM, my recommendation is that you and your legal team apply the teachings my father has wonderfully poured into this work.

De'Andre Robbins

INTRODUCTION

What comes to mind when you think of a private investigator? The first private investigator you imagine wears a fashionable black leather jacket with a lot of pockets. Perhaps the image that comes to mind for you is a tall, dark-haired guy with a beige or brown trench coat and of course the brown hat tilted to the front. You may be more into the female private investigator who looks like all the ladies from the television drama *Charlie's Angels* rolled into one super detective.

I bet you even see your P.I. parked on a side street staking out a building with a high-power Canon camera and a special lens that is as big as the car window. Or are you sure all private investigators are like the Hawaii-based television detective *Magnum P.I.* living in a rich friend's mansion and driving a performance vehicle with friends who own nightclubs and helicopters? Your investigator archetype might look like the guy from the spinoff TV show *HAWK*. Tall, dark, bald, sporting the baddest full-length fur and leather coats with shades that look like they are custom designed.

Did I hit your idea of what an investigator looks like with those characters?

While we are discussing this, what do you think a professional private investigator does? That is a loaded question. Certainly, they do things like assist in locating missing people; finding assets a deadbeat parent might be hiding. And yes, they will help you get the hard evidence you need to bust a cheating spouse.

There is, however, a more specialized area of private investigation that you need to be aware of. My mission is to introduce you to this area and give you some solid counsel on how you can employ investigative wisdom in your own situations. Don't worry, I am not going to send you to websites like peoplefinders.com, tell you to get a nanny cam, or tell you how to cleverly tail the person you think your spouse is cheating with.

Before I get to the good stuff, let me tell you how I know what I know. That is one of the most critical things in criminal investigation, research and knowing who you are adding to your team. My father was a federal Drug Enforcement Administration agent. I grew up in a law enforcement family. I started out in the law enforcement field early in my career, but the politics of the field illuminated some gross differences in racial and cultural treatment of suspects, those arrested and those imprisoned. Ironically, when a personal situation arose in my career, the same department that I was fighting for and standing with not only turned its back on me; but did its best to embarrass me. I ended up having to defend myself in a criminal proceeding, which was later proven to be false and the matter was closed as unfounded. I gained a sharp and intimate view of both sides of the coin and have developed an ultra-professional multi-state firm to assist others. What I can tell you with certainty is that the investigator is the person that usually solves case whether for the prosecution or for the defense. They are the ones that do most of the work.

I was fortunate. I had the financial wherewithal to hire three lawyers with a professional and thorough investigator. Not everyone can say the same. The lack of funds leads more people to accepting what they shouldn't than you would imagine. Just what is this area of private investigative or private detective work I am carrying on about? Criminal investigation!

CHAPTER

1

WHAT CAN A CRIMINAL DEFENSE INVESTIGATOR DO FOR ME?

I made a bold statement earlier; some may have even found it a bit arrogant. Yet, I stand by it: "the investigator is the person that usually solves cases whether for the prosecution or for the defense." Most people buy into the notion that the attorney wins the case based on what is argued in court. That's not necessarily factual, the attorney is your advocate for representation according to legal statutes. A criminal defense investigator is not only going to have their client's best interest and favorable outcome in mind but also proving what law enforcement has presented to be — well — suspect. A lawyer may recommend a private investigator if it is clear the law enforcement investigation may have left some stones untouched; or their perspective is dramatically skewing information from a crime scene, forensic or other information. So, criminal investigators also have the unique mission of assessing the client's criminal matter and how police detectives assessed the case.

Criminal defense investigations go as far back as the mid-18th century when those in the profession where primarily known as private detectives. Criminal defense investigation is a specialized skill set requiring knowledge of basic law enforcement techniques and strategies, as well as advanced study of policing tactics. The overall and most critical objective of the criminal defense investigator is TRUTH. Seek TRUTH. Uncover TRUTH. Challenge assumed TRUTH. To do this, they must negate all biases, question all evidence, consider everyone with information an important key to the case. Years ago, the television show *Perry Mason* painted the relationship between a criminal defense investigator and the defense attorney vividly. Mason always had a professional investigator who made it his business to find witnesses, information and disconnections in the prosecutor's case. That's part of a CDIs role — diligently pull those things that support reasonable doubt in a matter to the forefront on behalf of the defense's case.

To serve the attorney, client and case most effectively, emotional distance must be established and maintained; a CDI who is easy to anger, easy to jump to conclusions, and swayed by the emotions of others loses the power of objectivity. Are you concerned about your client and the outcome of their case? Absolutely! But, in a professional manner. Emotions, opinions, and bias cloud identifying each avenue of possibility that should be explored.

A criminal defense investigator can be employed to assist in varying criminal cases. Let's explore a few of them so you have a broader idea of how an investigator can be critical to your team. This is not an exhaustive list, but one provided to open your eyes; and remind you that professional criminal and private investigators do more than follow cheating spouses. You'd be surprised how many people find themselves the center of attention, suspect, or charged in local, state or federal investigations in one of these areas.

- Domestic and International Terrorism
- Arson
- Murder/Homicide/Attempted Murder
- Rape/Statutory Rape
- Kidnapping and Human/Sexual Trafficking
- Assault and battery
- Piracy on the water and electronic piracy of sensitive or financial data
- Tax fraud

A criminal defense investigator is a suspense novel writer. While most of us do not actually write novels, we are looking at the story and determining how the story can be spun. The investigator and the opposing entity can be looking at the same information yet we're creating conflicting conversations or storylines. We are having a debate, if you will, advocating for one position against the other. What is going to help the defense's client is who is more convincing when telling the story through the records, evidence, witnesses, and research presented. And when the CDI is successful at weaving a story that illuminates alternate possibilities, reasonable doubt and better-suited suspects, then the defense attorney's role of relaying the story in court becomes easier.

The investigative techniques employed will vary based on a case, initial steps are centered on validating and tearing apart the law enforcement investigation. This could include examining the evidence assembled by prosecutors or the indicting agency, revisiting the crime scene, questioning priority witnesses or persons of interest, and examining records, or identifying which records were overlooked. A critical point to remember when posturing yourself for success in your criminal case is that police detective work is not flawless. There will be missteps, overlooks, not mentioned or not investigated probabilities. In far too many instances, police zero in on a suspect and move full steam ahead on gathering enough to prosecute a case against that suspect not necessarily presenting the full story.

You must understand that they are weaving the story they believe to be true, just like the defense. There can potentially be multiple sides to one story. The criminal defense investigator wants to assure their side and their story outshines them all. Witnesses play a starring role in these stories we are all weaving for the client or suspect or accused.

The detective on *Perry Mason* could always pull a rabbit out of the hat. He could find a witness that a whole police force never even looked for. That is what a thorough criminal defense investigator does — find those who were hiding in plain sight. Find those with a bit of information that can shift the story powerfully. They find the witnesses with some contradictory details about what the prosecutor or charging agency believes will win its case.

I know this is going to blow your mind — but - witnesses don't always tell the truth. And how about this — they don't always tell everything they know, especially if you don't ask the questions that pull what they know. You may be one of those people that watch all the investigative news and documentary shows: *The First 48, Dateline, Unsolved Mysteries* and so many others. If you are, you know law enforcement will often chase a trail based on what a witness says. A CDI must evaluate the sincerity, legitimacy and accuracy of a witness and then determine which trail we should follow.

The evaluation and representation of the witness can lead to dropped charges or lesser charges. An investigator can help the defense witness relay their information to a judge and jury with candor and their interpretation of the truth. A CDI then investigates a witness' background. Is there a record? Are there medical conditions? Is there mental illness? We have to be able to counter or deflect anything that can be used to the prosecution's advantage.

There are other things that impact a witness' credibility and how a witness can be assessed or interviewed. If a potential witness is a child, their vocabulary or comprehension may be limited. The words used in the evaluation will have to be tailored to their age level or understanding level. If a potential witness is an older person you must weigh the capacity of their memory. Are there signs of Alzheimer's or dementia or other memory loss challenges? Older people for whom English is a second language may also experience translation and comprehension challenges. In these instances, an investigator needs to use extreme patience and build rapport to determine their most comfortable way of relaying information. Other key areas investigators must bear in mind when interviewing or determining witness credibility include a person's background, their relationship to the client or the opposing party, their mental state and their overall intellectual capacity.

While that sounds simple, interviewing and assessing witnesses requires interrogation training and experience. The investigator is not just listening for what a witness knows or will discuss, but also those things police officers didn't hear, didn't recognize as critical information or just didn't add to their reports. We're also interviewing to find out if proper procedures were used during the witness' time with police.

The investigator must be skilled in various interviewing strategies and able to determine which is most appropriate for the witness at the time. A long list of interview strategies can be used like kinesic (body language and non-verbal evaluation — the Wicklander Technique); cognitive (using four methods to help revisit the criminal occurrence); and behavioral analysis (weighing verbal and non-verbal responses against each other). Another key interview style is the "Reid Interrogation Technique". Developed by psychologist and polygraph expert John Reid more than 50 years ago, the technique is used to extract information from unwilling suspects, the Reid Technique is subject to error and has produced a large number of false confessions especially in juvenile cases.

Whichever technique is determined appropriate for the witness, it must be conducted without bias, without emotion and with an identified result in mind. These interviews are typically recorded and then chronicled in detailed reports.

Your criminal defense investigator must not only match but surpass law enforcement when it comes to having the confidence and people skills to gather what's needed for your case. In doing that, they still have to stay within the confines of legal statutes, polices and rules of procedure. Your CDI should also have working knowledge and experience with blood stains and patterns, weaponry, forensic terms, crime scene reconstruction, and procedures for collecting evidence, and — if applicable — understanding autopsy reports.

What I want you to understand is your case is critical. Your life hinges on what can be discovered, uncovered and revealed by both teams. The criminal investigator on your team must be top-notch and fully confident in what they know and who they know. Everyone needs a network of people in various places who provide additional investigative services or serve as professional or expert witnesses. Always consider who your defense investigative team has in their pocket.

Even with all this experience and knowledge, the most vital component and part of the defense team is you. Your role as a criminal defense investigator in your matter can help or hinder your team. With that in mind, follow their lead, always practice discretion with everyone, even those you've known for years. Why? Everyone can be swayed in these various stories swirling during an investigation. What you say can bolster one storyline against the other. Be available to be present and active in the investigation, a missing client makes the story a nightmare.

CHAPTER
2

IDENTIFYING RACIAL BIAS

Don't tell anyone this. Even if you do, they will strongly disagree with you. But we all have some cultural or racial biases. We look at someone and make assumptions, judgements or determinations based on our beliefs about who and what we see. That is bias. Bias means we have certain inclinations or what we hold to be verifiable predispositions about specific people or groups of people. The same holds true in law enforcement and criminal investigation. Black men — and even women — are more likely to be viewed as dangerous or violent. In some areas, Latin men are predetermined to be gang members. After 2016, and due to political influences, Mexican men were predominantly seen as thieves and rapists. All these listed are also presumed to be lower income, have had some history with the legal system and abuse drugs or alcohol.

These preconceived notions are called implicit bias. Implicit bias is defined as "an automatic and unintentional process that occurs in the human mind, and it affects how we respond to various groups in divergent ways and that those different and divergent responses can have unfortunate consequences." (Oxford Dictionary)

Implicit bias is also programmed and accidental. What I mean is some are programmed to have a natural disregard or disrespect for a culture of people based on their upbringing, their community or the environment around them. Some of us are accidentally programmed to have these biases. After the terrorist attack on the World Trade Center on September 11, 2001, many of us grabbed hold to the notion that anyone from the Middle East was a terrorist. We began to fear or at least look at our hijab-wearing co-worker a bit differently. It was not intentional, but the messaging on global media perpetrated and supported that bias.

We cycle what happened to someone by someone who looks a particular way in our brain, and it influences how we react to various gatherings and people in unique manners. Sometimes those manners are violent; depressing and create emotional and mental harm. Sadly, I must admit something you already know. This is especially true in law enforcement and in our legal and judicial systems. Implicit biases and blatant racism and cultural fears play a critical part in how these entities will respond to your case and what charges they will choose to levy against you.

I get it. We prefer to accept that we are a nation that looks to the standard of law and that the standard of law is genuinely applied to all fragments of society. However, can we look at the alarming and growing incidents reported by global media and hold true to that? We've had more than sufficient proof over the last decade or so to understand that bias effects the framework of equity and equality when it comes to who will be charged and how, who will be approached aggressively or violently by law enforcement and who will face harsher sentences. If you are anything except middle to upper class Anglo American you must understand that racial, cultural and social biases are at work in your case. Those biases will absolutely determine what type of professional concern will go into your investigation. Those biases carry a hefty weight on the assumption of your guilt, in some instances even more than the evidence and witnesses.

You cannot have blinders on about implicit bias as a person of color or a different culture. If your culture is one that speaks loudly and excitedly, when you speak out of your cultural norm to a police officer or investigator you are deemed as aggressive. If you have the tendency to move or pace when you are nervous you are seen as a physical threat. Whether it is a jury member, a prosecutor, your attorney, or police investigators they all are making decisions from their predispositions about your skin, gender, culture and socioeconomic status.

After slavery was abolished in 1865, Southern parts of the United States, where more than 90% of Blacks lived, adopted and established specific criminal justice measures as a means of racial control. Discriminatory "Black Codes" led to unprecedented numbers of people of color suffering through continuing slave-like conditions and treatments. The United States has the highest incarceration rate; and it is believed, and shown in numerous criminal justice research projects, that most of those imprisoned were convicted in cases fueled by prejudice, bias and implicit bias. In highly imbalanced numbers, minorities continue to be arrested more and are charged more severely. This indicates that the bias is a festering legal and judicial system sore. So, you must be mindful to enter your investigation with eyes wide open knowing what's perceived by law-enforcement may not be accurate and may be based on their opinions of those who look like you.

So, what can be done about this? Because I am clearly telling you that aside from worrying about if the evidence they have against you is circumstantial and substantial — bias is at play. I am saying that while you are working with your criminal defense investigator to find truths and shatter lies from witnesses — bias is at play. I am telling you that if you are involved in a criminal case with someone who is white — bias will be in play and you will be the major person of interest in the matter.

If your criminal matter involves child abuse allegations, cultural understandings will not be taken into consideration, however bias from caseworkers and departments will. If you are Muslim, your spiritual practices might dictate there are certain things you're not going to do with your kid that a Christian family might do with their child. If you're Buddhist, there are certain things you want to do with your kids that a Muslim person's not going to do with theirs. You can't rely on caseworkers, investigators or other professionals to have enough training or cultural empathy or awareness to assess a situation through a different lens. That's where your personal investigation must suggest alternatives to the points of view filed or reported. Implicit bias, racism, and culturalism is the other line of concern you must give full attention to.

When Hurricane Katrina destroyed parts of Louisiana in August 2005 there were heartbreaking images of people being rescued, flooded homes, and people fleeing the city. There were also images of people moving in and out of damaged stores and homes carrying various items. Were they gathering things from their own homes, or the homes of a family member or friend? Were they grabbing necessities aware that they had no means to replace them? Were they looting? Some likely were, some out of necessity, others out of greed. However, without investigating each occurrence thoroughly, the messaging describing what was going on showed America's inherent biases. Black people wading in water carrying items was described as "looting," while other photos showing white people in comparable situations was described as "carrying items." When predominantly white crowds, turned over vehicles, set fires, threw bottles and other items and trashed streets and stores after a victorious sports season the descriptions were over-zealous, over-the-top celebrations. When Black and mixed-race crowds did the same after police-involved questionable killings the terms used were riots, thugs, trashing. Same activities different biased terms.

What are some strategies we can use to interrupt and transform biases? From the legal side, training and testing modules must be developed to address potentially unconscious racial prejudices in interactions. There also must be increased terminations of blatantly racist and prejudiced officers, investigators and officers of the court.

Other strategies for interrupting biases are:

- Be aware of your biases and those around you
- Be motivated to shift your biases
- Be trained in multi-cultural, multi-ethnic, multi-religious and multi-social economic philosophies and behaviors
- Seek diverse contacts who can help you think broader
- Stay accountable to yourself and who you serve in changing your biases

The large takeaway here is that everyone has predispositions. We must recognize them and develop answers and new mindsets to disturb them.

CHAPTER
3

THE
INVESTIGATION

L ife is full of surprises. One moment you are enjoying your freedom and rights as an American citizen or resident; the next minute, everything is stripped away because you've committed (or are accused of committing) a criminal offense. Some people commit these unlawful acts knowingly while others happen by accident. That means you need to know how to posture yourself and act during your criminal case investigation to increase your chances of winning the case.

Criminal cases can end up in state or federal court. The main difference is federal investigators do far more exhaustive work in evidence discovery, witness research and other investigative techniques. If your case lands on the federal level, be forewarned your team is going to have Goliath-sized opponents. Determining whether a case ends up in federal court depends on a range of factors. In example, if you are accused of kidnapping someone in Florida; and decide for some reason to drive to Georgia; once you cross state lines while committing or while being accused or suspected of committing a crime your case becomes a federal matter. The Pew Research Center conducted a survey to determine the success rate of federal criminal cases. The report indicated that there were 80,000 federal defendants in 2018, but only 1,600 of them went to trial. Ninety percent of them pleaded guilty as charged, while 8% were acquitted. The report also indicated that only 320 defendants who went to trial managed to win their cases.

These numbers show that there are slim chances of proving your innocence after your criminal case has reached the federal courts. However, the way you posture yourself during the investigation process can make all the difference. Before we dive into that, let's first understand the different criminal cases and their investigation processes.

Investigating Homicide Cases

A surveillance report by Statista showed that there were 16,425 reported homicide cases in the United States in 2019. That represented a significant decrease since 2017, when the total number of murders and manslaughter cases were 17,294.

Former New York and Florida homicide detective David Waksman, who teaches homicide investigation techniques, tells the story of a horrendous homicide in South Florida's Miami Gardens area. The homicide took place in 1977 when the area was known as Carol City, a middle class Black neighborhood. Six people were murdered, five of them were positioned like spokes on a bicycle and executed. Police, acting on a tip, were able to identify the gunmen while convincing the person who drove the getaway car to testify. With that tip, and someone with factual and key information, three men were convicted and sentenced to death.

After a homicide case is reported, police officers and investigators usually move quickly to secure the crime scene and gather critical evidence. In Waksman's case they were able to find bullet shells that were from the same gun used to kill an elderly couple months earlier. They were also able to tie the same suspects to a third murder when it was determined the gun used in that incident was stolen from the home where the six people were killed. The suspects inadvertently (and a bit arrogantly) were connecting dots to three horrific crimes. These are the types of things detectives look for and the types of things a criminal defense investigator will also look for if you find yourself accused in a homicide case. Documentation is the primary role of everyone involved in the investigation process, from the first police officer on the scene, to the lead investigator, to the evidence technicians and others. They will usually ask questions such as:

- What did you do?
- What did you see?
- When did you do this or that?
- What did you hear?

Those questioned are required to answer these questions from their personal point of view, allowing pieces of information that are essential and may offer leads or further insight into the homicide case to be revealed.

When investigating criminal matters, specifically homicide cases, it's imperative that you have basic knowledge of autopsy reports, entry and exit wounds, and cause of death terminology. You also want to review the crime scene report, crime scene photos and any blood patterns that may be evident.

It's important to learn to speak to the dead, not literally but to the evidence that may be around them. So, recanvas your scene, do not just accept what the police have reported. Retrace everything they have done to find that one piece of missing evidence or that one overlooked witness. Your job is to leave no rock unturned.

Request to see and examine the murder weapon if one exists, have the attorney obtain an order for you to examine the evidence, it's important for you to know what the police know. If there were body cameras worn in an officer-involved incident or by officers during the investigation, request the footage from every officer on the scene, pull the 911 call, and you may even want to interview the medical examiner. Skilled investigators, like the professional you'll have on your team, may also do a computer recreation of the crime scene, looking for multiple and alternative ways the person could have died.

Investigating Domestic Violent Cases

A data report by the National Coalition Against Domestic Violence revealed that one in four women and one out of nine men experience some form of domestic violence resulting in physical injuries, emotional distress, fearfulness, and post-traumatic stress disorder (PTSD). In one year, over 10

million Americans became victims of domestic violence. The investigation will follow several standard procedures.

- **Documentation** – The first responding officer will take photographs by camera or smartphone to reveal the extent of physical injuries suffered by the victims. Usually, they [victims] appear in court with improved health. Relying on their appearance at the time can harm your case. Photographs also express the victim's emotional state and help in showing things that the officer may fail to indicate in the report.

- **Finding witnesses** – An investigator's chances of taking your domestic violence case to court improve by about 70% when they find witnesses. These may include the individual(s) who called 911 to report the crime, neighbors, or the children at home.

- **Obtaining Protective Order** – The investigating officer can retrieve an emergency protective order (EPO). The officer takes the case report to the judge before issuing it to the prosecutor. If the judge sees enough evidence that warrants trial, he will provide a protective order. That hedges the prosecution's case against external influences that may deter the case's advancement.

- **Making Arrests** – The arrest of a domestic violence suspect increases the probability of prosecution and conviction by 96% and 80%, respectively. Furthermore, case filing rates double when law enforcement makes an arrest. Once in police custody, they have a limited timeframe to take the case to court.

- **Multiple Offenses/Crimes** – The responding officer or investigator will usually be quick to look for other reasons to include other charges in their report. If the statement reports that more than one crime was committed, your chances of heading to trial jump significantly, by 300%.

The key to winning domestic or intimate partner violence cases mirror some of the steps in homicide cases. Namely, re-canvassing the scene where the abuse took place, re-interviewing all witnesses and talking to the victim again. Domestic violence cases are unpredictable because they are centered on matters of the heart. Be emphatic and sympathetic to the victim, and build a rapport allowing them to feel more comfortable in speaking with you. Bear in mind, there are instances where victims are not telling the truth. While it may seem harsh, part of your personal investigation and definitely that of a criminal defense investigator will focus on the victim's background. This background check may include social media posts, prior police reports and their social and lifestyle habits. As you build your defense, think of these standard questions:

- What was the victim's reason for calling police?
- Are there any bruises present?
- Who called the police?
- Were there any witnesses to the incident?

A good investigator will also pull an address grid which allows you to see how many times the police have been called out to the address on similar matters. Also, consider running a name search to find out how many times the victim (or the alleged abuser) was involved with police. A good criminal investigator will also work on the premise that everyone is lying. That investigator will also work towards getting the victim to recant their story or obtain a written statement hopefully contradicting the one provided to the police.

Investigating Financial Crimes

One of the reasons law enforcement has a financial investigation system is to hunt down criminals and other organized groups who engage in financial fraud, embezzlement or a number of other crimes where money is the enterprise. The essence is to target the financial proceeds from their criminal activities to ensure they do not have the necessary resources to further their criminal pursuits. These cases are strongly argued around bank records and mountains of other financial records. In many cases, a detailed review of these is done through a forensic audit by an independent accounting firm.

Financial crime investigators usually conduct both financial and criminal case investigations to determine the financial benefits obtained due to indulgence in a specific criminal activity. Law enforcement officers, officials from the justice department, financial institutions, and the Financial Intelligence Unit may get involved in the investigation process to ensure that they leave no stone unturned. The bottom line is not to believe the numbers until the numbers have been broken down and evaluated multiple times; and you have FOLLOWED THE MONEY, down to the last cent

CHAPTER

4

INVESTIGATING
CHILD
WELFARE
(DCF) CASES

*On at least a few occasions, the father has spoken very sexually,
always about how pretty baby "p____" is and how "sweet it tastes".
He gave descriptions about how tiny the clitoris is, especially when
they are "youngins". He described how the penetration felt and all.
At an unknown time, when the father was seen with his child, he had
an erection as she was standing between his legs. He was moving
her body against his.*

When law enforcement agencies receive a report of child negligence or abuse like this one, they must investigate. Different entities can be involved in the process. However, it is typically Child Protective Services (CPS) or the Department of Children and Families (DCF) that head the investigation. The reason for an investigation is to obviously determine whether a minor is at risk of danger or harm, minimize any risk, get the child to safety if there is legitimate and proven harm; or in some instances offer social services and mental and emotional support to the family.

Child abuse cases can be difficult to navigate. Sadly, accusations and reports are often filed out of discontent, failed relationships, jealousy, general dislike and other emotionally driven circumstances. These reported incidents are largely found to be false and cases are closed. Likewise – and sadly – there are instances where there is abuse, yet parental or other influencers pressure or harass a victim into denying the abuse claims. There were two daughters who moved to a new state away from the family they had grown up with and were living with their mother and stepfather. On the first day of their new arrangements, the stepdad inappropriately kissed one of the daughters. He then went on to improperly touch and kiss both for about a year, before one of the daughters threatened to say something. Before she could, the other daughter wrote about their plight in a story for school. Police and CPS were called in. The day the daughter was scheduled to go the police station and talk to detectives, the stepfather threatened her. He told her if she said anything to them, she and her mom and sister would be on the streets and he would take everything they had. That was terrifying for a 10-year old. She told authorities the story was something she made up. They closed the investigation.

Anyone can call legal authorities and provide tips about the sexual, physical or other abuse of a child. They do not need to be a family member, a medical professional or someone in the child's education community. Your neighbor can become increasingly angry because your family makes a bit too much noise enjoying time in the pool and call and report that he's seen you fondling your child or trying to drown them in the pool. Your ex-partner's sister can decide you are wrong in your decision to not allow the kids to spend Christmas with their side of the family, and file a report indicating you have kidnapped the children. They may even file a missing person's report, knowing that you denied the request for that holiday visit because you were taking them to Disneyland. Just like that – you are subject to an abuse of a minor criminal investigation. As with domestic violence cases, the investigators will document any physical and emotional abuse by taking photographs. They'll also gather any other evidence that indicates signs of child neglect. They will talk to school officials and anyone else in regular communication or connection with the child and your family.

There is a tremendous amount of bias in these types of investigations. The U.S. Department of Health reports that minority children, and in particular African American children, are more likely to end up in foster care placement than receive in-home help services. Sadly, that same report found this to be true even when black children are incurring the same problems and displaying the same characteristics as white children.

Another instance of bias in these types of cases is what you are told about the reporting of an incident. The detailed report filed by Child Protective Services or intake entity is confidential. You are not advised who filed the report or on what grounds they filed the report. The police report is not confidential; it is public record. So, if law enforcement gets involved, you then have legal access to the report filed. There is still information that may be redacted (blacked out) to protect the integrity of the investigation and the child. Additionally, we talked about a good investigator being able to tell a convincing story, in these cases, a good investigator must give a keen eye to finding the conflicts in the story. They must expose the possibilities of a false report being filed and assure those things are entered into the investigative files. As with so many areas of the criminal system, African American, Haitians and other Caribbean people of color, and poor whites are amongst the highest number of cases that end up the child abuse system.

A large part of this is due to cultural differences and misinterpretations. Even when counseling professionals are pulled in to question a child, the language of a community can be misinterpreted. Therefore, as part of your investigation, you want to assure that your child can speak with someone who is trained in dealing more effectively with multiple cultures. Without money to hire your own counselor this can be difficult but be diligent in pushing for it.

I have seen so many cases where this has played out to the detriment of the accused. I recall a case where accusations were made against a man who owned a daycare center with his wife. They arrested him for child molestation stating that he regularly touched the kids. I went to the guy in jail, looked him in the eyes, and asked, "Did you do it?" He said, "Man, I have never touched a kid in my life. I don't even know what they are talking about." The critical question showed where cultural terminology led to an arrest. I asked, "What did you tell the police officer?"

He said, "The only thing I told them was that the one little girl they asked me about was acting up and I grabbed her, to keep her calm." They took the word grabbed and ran with it. On the recording of his interrogation, they ask, "Is there any way possible that while she was moving around, she could have rubbed against you?" He said, "Anything is possible. I don't believe so, but it's possible." I understood what he was trying to say; honestly, anybody with common sense should have understood, but they took that as probable cause to make an arrest. In investigating the case, I discovered the child's mom was trying to get some money from the owners to help with the cost of treatment for the child's mental issues.

The mom had confessed to a medical professional that she had a problem with the family because of the little girl's behavior. She told other people on the street around their neighborhood that the man never did anything. Eventually, we were able to corroborate their story by getting third party evidence of people that the mom talked to. Nevertheless, in the process the daycare owners were raked over the coals in the media, based on the misinterpretation of language.

Transparently, I must say that there are abuse allegations that are true. Some of us may remember the popular television series *Good Times* that chronicled the happenings of a lower-class Black family in Chicago and their dreams and quests to get out of the ghetto. In a series of episodes, we met the character Penny. Penny was being abused by her mother. You may recall the show where the mother unplugged a clothes iron and approached her with it. The next episode marks and burns were seen on her body. The character Wilona called authorities. In that case, the mother was physically abusing the child and ended up abandoning her.

We've also seen the headlines of unbelievable cases of child abuse. There is the case of Timothy Ray Jones Jr. in South Carolina.

Police found high level drugs in his car during a police checkpoint. While in custody he took police to the bodies of his five children, who he had placed in garbage bags and thrown on the side of the road. This after driving several states with their bodies in the car. After a trip with the kids to Disney World, Jones said he was concerned his kids - all under nine - were going to kill him. He had custody of his kids after a nasty divorce.

There is the case of Josh Powell, who had lost custody of his two young sons to their maternal grandparents after he was accused of foul play in his wife's mysterious disappearance. His case even made it to the network criminal drama show *Dateline*. The kids were under Child Protective Services care and could see him in supervised visits at his residence. That didn't sit well with the grandparents, but the agency still allowed it. Two or three days after the court dealt him a blow in his bid to get the kids back, the case worker took the kids to the house for a visit. Powell grabbed the kids inside and locked the door, ignoring the caseworker's demands to open the door and return the kids immediately. Hours later, Powell and both boys were killed in a well-orchestrated explosion by Powell.

There are some things you must understand about the nature of these types of abuse investigations. Child protective investigators can pull your child out of class and question them without your permission and without notifying you in advance. They can also do the same at a center where your child might be involved in sports or some other extracurricular activity. They have the legal right to do that. This is often the case when a case worker may feel family members are not being forthcoming with information. In my experience with these types of cases, there are clear instances when abuse is happening, but because sexual or physical abuse is woven into the family's dynamics; every allegation is denied by those who are keenly aware of what is going on. Victims are then quieted and become part of an unfortunate and violent cycle.

Thus, case workers or investigators may show up at family homes or where abuse is reportedly taking place without warning. They have the legal right to show up at your home without an appointment to interview you and the child(ren) in question. Read this part very carefully. You DO NOT have to let them in. Case workers can't see you without a warrant. They don't have the right to enter your home. You can stop them at the front door. The mistake many people make is responding positively when asked if they can come in; or inviting them in. Once you give them entry and access, if they see something in the house that's not appropriate, since you invited them in, they can evaluate some things without needing a warrant.

Should they show up, step outside to speak with them. If they want to question you, ask them what the allegations against you are. Let them know you would like to have the conversation recorded and ask is there any way possible that you can have your attorney present. You can relay to them something similar to this, "I'll be more than happy to speak with you, but right now I think I need someone on my side to help me be able to make sure that you don't misinterpret what I'm saying." From there ask to reschedule the questioning for a time your attorney can be present. This way you are (1) cooperating; (2) gathering information; and (3) protecting your rights.

If you choose to speak with them, and I strongly recommend you do not without someone there to witness the conversation, record it. Use whatever recording app you have on your cell phone or a tablet if you have one handy. But do not start talking before you know what they're accusing you of! Then you turn the questioning on them. Ask: Where did the allegation come from? How long ago was this? Was it recent? Give me a time frame, please. These are critical questions they can provide responses to. You can ask: What's the allegation specifically? What day did I allegedly do this? If they spoke to your child at school, you may also speak to and ask questions of the administrator who was present during the questioning. Because it is a child, an administrator has to be on hand to function as a guardian. Ask the principal, counselor or other administrator: Was the discussion with the investigator recorded? Who else was present during the discussion? What time did the case investigator come? Did they get the name of the person questioning your child? What information did they provide?

Whether you launch out as your own investigator in a child abuse case or hire someone to help you; everything I'm sharing with you is information you need to know. There is a point I touched on before that I want to assure you do not miss. If it is considered public record you may access it and get a copy of it. There are fees in some jurisdictions for those copies, but you still have access to them. Public records are most court case listings (known as dockets), police reports, 911 call transcripts. You also have a right to your DCF or CPS file; although they may not release it until the case is fully passed on judicially or otherwise closed.

One of the most difficult parts of these cases is watching the lives of people who were accused yet were genuinely innocent unravel. Investigations can spill over into various areas of one's life leaving a trail of doubt, lingering questions and negativity — especially if it is a case that found itself in the media. And as exhaustive as investigations by child protective workers can be, when you are exonerated or it is determined the charges were unfounded, you are likely going to get something with one sentence: **There is no evidence to support the allegations.** There will be no retraction or update to the media story. It is very unlikely that the school or the child's doctor will be notified. That dirty mark, though wrongly applied, will be there. Remain encouraged and work on repairing whatever discord may have entered your family and get counseling if necessary. This is especially necessary for a child who found themselves amid something that is terribly intimidating and confusing. Like my grandma used to always tell me, people remember the negative over the positive every time.

If you are guilty of the allegations, avoid putting your family and the child through more examinations, interrogations and scrutiny than necessary. For the safety of your child allow child protective services to quietly remove him or her from the home. In most instances, if they determine the child will be safe, they will try to place them with a family member. It may be distressing but imagine the distress the child you have abused is feeling. The ultimate thing for a criminal defense investigator in child abuse cases is to protect the child and to help clear a client who is wrongly accused.

CHAPTER

5

REPORT
WRITING AND
EVIDENCE
DOCUMENTATION

To improve your chances of winning a criminal case, you need to compile a report and provide evidence about what took place. That said, you need to have answers to the five Ws [and one H]; much like newspaper and magazine reporters are told to present in their stories. Those are: What, When, Where, Who, Why, and How. There are six questions that are asked when writing a criminal case report. They help in breaking down a complicated case into morsels of details for better understanding. If you conduct your own criminal investigation, these questions will need to be addressed.

- **What happened?** This involves inquiries into the sequence of events that occurred and the actions of those involved in the crime.

- **When did the crime take place?** When it comes to interpersonal criminal cases, such as domestic violence and financial fraud, the victim may remember the exact time that the suspected crime happened.

- **Where did the crime happen?** Sometimes a crime can occur in multiple locations. For instance, after getting involved in financial crime, an alleged offender may be compelled to indulge in money laundering activities in another business. Knowing these locations can help explain motive.

- **Who participated in the crime?** In a criminal case, there is always an offender. There can also be one or more victims, witnesses, and third parties. They can provide more precise information about the involved persons when writing the statements.

- **Why did they act like that?** It is critical to understand the reasons that made the offender act in the way they did. In cases like theft, the motive is often straightforward. Domestic violence and homicide cases often require investigators to dig a lot deeper to understand the reason for committing the crime.

- **How did the crime take place?** In every stage of a crime, the offender must make decisions, work with others, and use specific tools and equipment. Even in a heat-of-the-moment crime, there was a sequence of events.

How to Properly Secure Affidavits from Witnesses and Victims

If you've watched any crime investigation TV series, you've heard witnesses in court say that they promise to "tell the truth and nothing but the truth." The lawyers often reiterate to witnesses and victims "remember that you are under oath." We can't mention that without talking about affidavits.

An affidavit is the written version of swearing under oath, just as you would when a witness is in a court of law. The document is often signed by the person making the statement, often known as an affiant, and by the legal professional administering the oath. If you are doing some investigating of your own you can get affidavit forms from the courts, attorneys, or financial institutions. Criminal defense investigators working with your defense team may draft a specific affidavit to legally record what is going to benefit the case.

Any individual determined to be a victim or witness to a crime can sign or attest to an affidavit, if they have the mental capacity to do so and are of legal age. The content of the affidavit is an indication of the affiant's personal knowledge of the case. That means that they cannot be prosecuted for omitting any details that they were not aware of.

There are various situations where an affidavit can be drawn up during a criminal trial process. For instance, for a witness to identify a suspected offender who has been at large for a considerable time.

An affidavit form will contain four crucial sections. These include:

1. A statement that the witness or victim is swearing under oath according to the guidelines and truthfulness detailed in the affidavit form.
2. In-depth details of what is being sworn to
3. The affiant's signature
4. Approval by a notary public or any other authorized entity that administers oaths

Understanding the Chain of Custody

In criminal law, chain of custody refers to the order in which the evidence is handled during the investigation of a case. Proving that an item has been properly handled through the unbroken chain of custody is required for it to be registered and presented as legal evidence during a trial or hearing. In criminal trials the prosecution must prove that all evidence was handled according to a properly documented and uninterrupted chain of custody; meaning if packaged cocaine seized in a drug bust is to go to evidence for weighing and tagging, then that is the chain of custody. If a detective or someone else places the cocaine in an unmarked file cabinet before it goes to evidence, then the chain of custody was disrupted and the documentation of what was seized and what was tagged is then questionable. Crime-related items found not to have followed a properly documented and unbroken chain of custody may not be allowed as evidence in trial. While often unnoticed outside of the courthouse, a thorough chain of custody has been a crucial factor in high profile cases, including the 1994 murder trial of former professional football star OJ Simpson. In this case, a piece of evidence was not properly sized or matched to the defendant, and as we all heard the late attorney Johnny Cochran proclaim, "if the glove does not fit you must acquit!"

A CDI should have a deep understanding of the prosecution's chain of custody to assist in establishing reasonable doubt of guilt. Your case can then be argued, presenting some loopholes and mishandling of the evidence-gathering process. For instance, the defense can claim, with facts, that the item was fraudulently planted to strongly point to guilt.

The chain of custody must have a companion document that highlights how the evidence item changed hands from the time it was retrieved from the crime scene to the time it is presented in court. Therefore, the Chain of Custody form must be signed by the police officers involved, forensic technicians analyzing the evidence, and the evidence technician who stores the evidence at the police precinct.

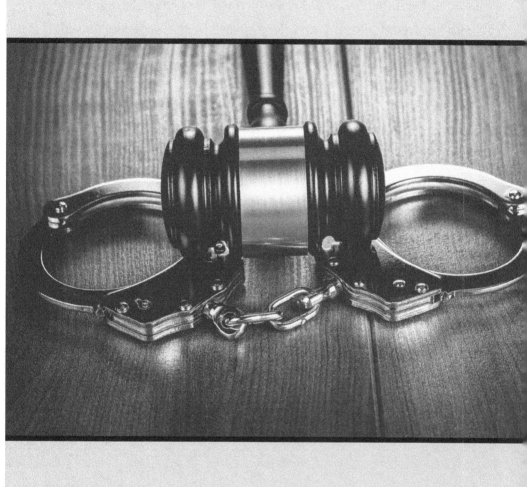

CHAPTER

6

TESTIFYING
IN COURT

A nytime a crime victim or witness is called to testify in court, they become an object of scrutiny. The judge, attorneys, jurors, and the audience are closely following what they have to say, how they say it, and how they look. It is critical to learn court etiquette and understand what's required of you, whether you are witnessing for the first or sixth time.

Dress and Act Appropriately

The way you dress, and look, says a lot about you in court. Sometimes the credibility of your statement is hinged on how you dress and body movements. Imagine a witness walking towards the stand with their pants hanging hip level; or wearing a white tank top with jeans, or even wearing a t-shirt that reads something derogatory like "Murder Is Always An Option." Chances are you—if you are on trial—have lost the respect of the judge and the jury. The way you dressed and walked into the courtroom implies you have disrespect for the judicial process. It also says that you are not taking the matter seriously. The same holds true if you go to court drunk or under the influence of drugs. If the court has not acknowledged that you have a speech impediment and provided the information to the jury, your slurred speech announces your condition. Both scenarios are unacceptable for a client and for a witness.

A witness must be even more presentable than the person on trial. Why? Because their presentation will give the jury confidence about their maturity, integrity and respect of the legal process. It also helps if the body language is in check. Slouching in a chair, not giving your full attention to the judge, attorney and jurors, sitting with your arms folded tight across your chest and rolling your eyes are all horrible posturing in the courtroom. Go to court well-dressed, clean, sober, respectful and with a professional mindset. Doing so is not farfetched, old-fashioned, or stupid. Your charges—or case—may already create an air of prejudice against you, your presentation or the presentation of your witnesses can subconsciously shift that—even if you're guilty. Dress like you would when attending a job interview.

Be Prepared. Know Your Case

Before you step into a courtroom, your attorney will prepare you in several ways; some may anger you. Years ago, in a personal divorce matter, my attorney would drill me and drill me in ways that nearly convinced me she did not have my best interest at heart and that she did not think I deserved to gain my desires in court. She explained that when we step into the courtroom, opposing counsel was going to hit me even harder than she

had, and her intent was to prepare me for it. The preparation helps a witness and a client to stay focused on the facts of the case that your attorney will present. The preparation also helps to manage emotions that may arise during the cross-examination phase. It also gives you some insight on how to respond to questions that may not have been introduced as possibilities by your counsel. A criminal defense investigator is a powerful tool to have in this regard. Their questioning style is going to be vastly different from your attorney's, whose role is to advocate for you. So, their techniques help the attorney present stronger testimonies from the client and supporting witnesses.

When it comes to answering questions, it is important that you answer every question posed to you thoroughly but briefly and without adding any other details. You need not explain the answer in detail for five minutes. If the query calls for a simple "yes" or "no" answer, then that's all you need to say. Avoid volunteering details unless your attorney or the judge directs you to. If you are asked: where were you on the night of November 14, 2019? you can say you attended a social function in downtown Memphis. You do not have to say that you were at a party at the X Hotel on Morris Street thrown by John Doe. You are volunteering more information than asked in that question. Allow questions to be posed before you provide details or comprehensive information that may not have been on their radar. Short, sweet, and as discussed with your team, is the only response strategy you should use.

It is also important that you open your mouth and speak clearly when responding to questions. Jurors will not hear competent statements if you are mumbling. The use of slang and jargon might sound like a foreign language to jurors, so it's best to use common English or if you speak an actual foreign language, make sure your attorney has requested and vetted a professional translator.

Establish Credibility

Anyone appearing on a court's witness stand is always nervous because they are the case's voice. The jury is expecting them to be prepared and have the facts about the case right. Without preparation, confidence plummets, and that's when you may start providing information that is inconsistent with what is in the affidavit or any other previous deposition.

Try to establish credibility with the jurors. Also, gather any documents or statements presented to the court and commit them to memory. Additionally, anticipate questions from the other party. That's easy, considering the known nature of the case. That way, the jury will know that whatever you are saying is credible and authentic.

CHAPTER

7

DON'T GO
IT ALONE

P rejudice, bias, weary law enforcement officers, exhausted protective and investigative entities—they are all lined up staring at your case and looking for your breaking point. The wise thing for anyone who finds themselves in a criminal, child abuse, wrongful conviction or capital mitigation matter is to work with a criminal defense investigator who can stare down the opposing forces coming against you.

With over 20 years of experience in law enforcement, as an advocate for children and a social activist; I have seen some interesting and horrific cases. What I know for sure is that an attorney is a powerful advocate; but a criminal defense investigator is a power tool that can hammer down what caseworkers, agents, detectives and others bring to the table. Don't make the critical mistake of thinking that hiring a private investigator that specializes in cases like yours is relegated to those with big cases, big money or big positions. You have the same access and the same rights to challenge the evidence, reports and witnesses against you. It's best to do that with someone who is an expert at retelling the story the opposition has crafted.

If you are a client, or someone other than a skilled Criminal Defense Investigator, remember these key points:

1) You can ask your attorney to hire an investigator to assist in your case; or you can hire one to collaborate with your attorney.

2) You have the right to request any information that is considered public record including copies of 911 calls.

3) In DCF Child Welfare Cases, you have the right to ask a child protective services investigator to schedule a meeting with you so that your attorney can be present.

4) In DCF Child Welfare Cases, you have the right to deny them access to your home without the proper paperwork.

5) You have the right to refuse to speak to a police officer. Remember zero plus zero equals zero which means if you say nothing that can't add anything to what you said - so - keep your mouth quiet. Never speak to law enforcement without your attorney present

6) If testifying in court, be mindful of your responses. Only answer what you are asked and keep your responses short and to the point.

7) If you feel like there is some form of bias happening in your case, you are probably right; discuss it with your attorney and CDI to come up with some strategies to make it work to your advantage.

8) The courtroom is the stage where matters concerning your life will be decided. Show up in court dressed to impress, voicing responses intelligently and clearly, giving full eye and body attention always to the proceedings at hand.

9) A private investigator or criminal defense investigator can serve a crucial role in your matter. And no street knowledge or corner store attorneys can employ techniques, strategies and even long practiced magic to turn things around in your favor.

To contact Dr. Anthony L. Robbins

Visit
Anthony L. Robbins, P.A.
Private Investigator

www.anthonylrobbins.com

CALL
(786) 490-9461
(877) 446-1264

Email: info@anthonylrobbins.com

Follow Anthony L. Robbins, P.A., Private Investigator

 https://www.facebook.com/anthonylrobbinspa

 https://twitter.com/alrassociates

Printed in the USA
CPSIA information can be obtained
at www.ICGtesting.com
LVHW012007020624
782068LV00001B/132

9 781735 829548